✪ WEAPONS OF WAR
DESTROYERS
1945 TO TODAY

Smart Apple Media

© 2015 Smart Apple Media, an imprint of Black Rabbit Books
P.O. Box 3263, Mankato, Minnesota, 56002
www.blackrabbitbooks.com

Published by arrangement with Amber Books

Contributing authors: Chris Chant, Steve Crawford, Martin J. Dougherty,
Ian Hogg, Robert Jackson, Chris McNab, Michael Sharpe, Philip Trewhitt

Special thanks to series consultant Dr. Steve Potts

Photo credits: Art-Tech/Aerospace, Cody Images, Corbis, U.S. Department of Defense

Illustrations: © Art-Tech/Aerospace

Library of Congress Cataloging-in-Publication Data

Jackson, Robert, 1941-
Destroyers : 1945 to today / Robert Jackson.
pages cm. — (Weapons of war)
Includes index.
ISBN 978-1-62588-043-7
1. Destroyers (Warships) — History. I. Title.
V825.J33 2015
623.825'4--dc23
　　　　　　　　　　　　2013033332

Printed in the United States at Corporate Graphics,
North Mankato, Minnesota
PO1649
2-2014

9 8 7 6 5 4 3 2 1

CONTENTS

Introduction

Modern Destroyers

The modern destroyer is a multipurpose fighting ship designed to take on a variety of tasks in a fast-changing world.

Until relatively recently, all warships could engage all targets. In the "Age of Sail" (approximately 1500-1850), the only opponents faced by a wooden sailing ship were cannon-armed warships and armed merchants, or an armed military unit on shore. Specialist ammunition and techniques were available, but for the most part, the choice of weapons was a simple one — as many of the biggest guns a ship could carry. Defense was a matter of strong timbers, good sailing skills to deny the enemy a crippling shot, and powerful enough weapons to win the fight before too much damage was done.

However, modern technology has greatly

ARAGUAYA: see page 30

WEAPONS OF WAR

NITEROI CLASS: see page 51

complicated this equation. The development of the submarine and aircraft have increased the range of possible threats considerably, while the invention of guided missiles, torpedoes, and mines have made whole new forms of defense necessary.

DEFENSE AND ATTACK

A warship can be attacked in four general ways: gunfire, torpedoes, mines, and airborne weapons. The last category includes bombs and rockets delivered by helicopters and aircraft as well as missiles launched from the shore, other ships, aircraft or submarines. For the purposes of defense, it does not matter how the weapon is delivered; a torpedo will always attack from underwater no matter whether it is fired from a small boat, a submarine, or dropped from a helicopter; and a missile will always come in above sea level.

Conversely, the nature of the target is critical to the choice of weapon when on the offensive. Guns and missiles are of little use against a submarine while torpedoes cannot be fired at aircraft or land targets. Thus, a

LEANDER CLASS: see page 34

PRAT (EX-NORFOLK): see page 54

WEAPONS OF WAR

DUGUAY-TROUIN: see page 36

KONGO CLASS: see page 46

warship must carry weapons suitable for the targets it expects to engage and defenses tailored to the weapons that are likely to attack it, rather than the platforms they are launched from. In addition to weapons and defenses, a warship needs a number of

Engines and propulsion systems are bulky and subject to diminishing returns in terms of increased size versus vessel speed. An extremely fast vessel is expensive and must devote space to machinery that could be used for other systems. It will also go through fuel at a high rate, reducing range or requiring yet more internal space to be given over to mobility rather than fighting power.

Sensors and control systems are also vital. Radar guidance is important for weapon accuracy, while sonar is essential to give warning of a submarine in the vicinity. Without radar and other sensors, a vessel can only engage targets within visual range, and even then the chances of a hit are low. The loss of a critical sensor system can "mission kill" a warship, forcing it to abandon its mission and return to base for repairs even though its weapons and engines are intact.

SUPPORT SYSTEMS

In order to find targets, move, and fight, a warship requires many other support systems. The crew needs to eat and sleep, and have suitable work stations. They must be able to communicate within the vessel and to deliver reports and receive orders, to deal with casualties and damage to the ship, and staff the ship appropriately. A tight design that crams immense capability into the hull at the expense of crew comfort

other critical systems. A propulsion system and sufficient fuel to allow for a reasonable operating area are of course necessary.

EXETER: see page 37

WEAPONS OF WAR

KNOX: see page 45

may result in inefficiency during a long deployment as the personnel become fatigued and frustrated.

It has wisely been said that the groundwork for victory at sea is laid in procurement and design meetings, when the systems that go into a ship are decided and their layout is determined. Further advantage is gained — or lost — from doctrine and tactics. The support of other vessels and the procedures used in combat can cover a ship's weaknesses and exploit its strengths and vice versa.

The creation of an effective warship requires balancing all the relevant factors — weapons, defense, sensors, mobility, and crew support systems. It is not always obvious what the right answer to this equation should be, especially when the additional constraints of cost and the ability to upgrade the vessel throughout its lifetime are considered. It's also possible that the vessel may have to fulfill an entirely different role than the one it was designed for; a lot can change during the lifetime of a naval vessel.

Some of the warships in the following pages are specialist designs built around a single role or mission concept. Some are mulitrole vessels designed to meet a range of challenges whether operating alone or while escorting other ships.

OLIVER HAZARD PERRY: see page 52

DESTROYERS

Since World War II, the destroyer has evolved from a torpedo-armed, all-gun surface warfare vessel into a specialist anti-air or anti-submarine ship, capable either of independent operations for a short time or of operating as an escort in a task force. The losses suffered by the United Kingdom's destroyers during the Falklands War (1982) proved that the UK's minimally armed warships, which had been constructed that way to satisfy restraints imposed by the UK Treasury, were extremely vulnerable in a conventional war, let alone the nuclear scenarios proposed for any future conflict. Short-term action was taken to rectify some of their faults, and plans made to update them as they became due for refit, with the installation of close-range weapons a high priority.

A more capable modern destroyer design was the Spruance class, produced by the US, and optimized for anti-submarine warfare (ASW). Modifying the design for the anti-air role produced the Kidd class, which at the time of commissioning were the most powerfully-armed general-purpose destroyers in the world. As initially built, the Spruance class attracted criticism with regard to its light armament. The class later matured into an effective multirole platform, as it was fitted with better air defenses and greatly increased surface warfare capability.

SPRUANCE: see page 56

WEAPONS OF WAR

Lightweight Kevlar armor was also added, increasing an already large displacement, but it remained an expensive alternative to vessels designed from the outset to serve in this role. Some of the Spruance-class vessels were retrofitted with the Tomahawk cruise missile, discharged from vertical launchers, but not all the 31 ships received the necessary modifications, as it was deemed too expensive.

The Sovremenny class of destroyers was designed in the 1970s by the Soviet Union and was developed from a vessel intended to support amphibious operations. The class is optimized for surface action, although it carries heavy anti-air defenses. Soviet vessels of the Cold War era were expected to have to operate under the heavy air threat posed by US carrier forces. Armament is based on long-range surface-to-surface missiles backed up by 130mm guns. Surface-to-air missiles and two close-in weapon systems provide air defense, and there are both torpedoes and

ÁLVARO DE BAZÁN: see page 28

ARLEIGH BURKE: see page 31

an anti-submarine rocket launcher for ASW work. A single helicopter is also carried. The Sovremenny class is large for a destroyer type; some authorities term them cruisers instead. They remain active in the Russian and Chinese navies. The main missile battery can launch either conventional or nuclear warheads. The latter were primarily envisioned as useful against high-value targets such as a US carrier group during potential all-out war. The use of nuclear weapons at sea, rather than land use, was thought to be less likely to lead to nuclear escalation.

COLD WAR FRIGATES

Ever since the frigate was developed in the eighteenth century — when it was used mainly for reconnaissance and commerce raiding — it has formed an important element in the world's navies. Today, the name is applied to a wide variety of vessels, ranging from very expensive and highly specialized anti-submarine warfare ships such as the UK's Type 22, to cheaper ships like the US Navy's Knox class, designed to escort convoys and amphibious warfare task groups.

KRIVAK: see page 48

BRANDENBURG: see page 32

F 215

WEAPONS OF WAR

UDALOY: see page 59

The frigate was an important part of the warship inventories of nations in both the east and west during the Cold War. The British Leander class of general purpose frigate, for example, which entered service in the 1960s, served well for many years. They were succeeded by the Type 22 Broadsword class, designed as ASW ships for the Greenland-Iceland-UK gap against Soviet high-performance nuclear submarines. The other principal British frigate is the Type 21 Amazon class, of which eight were built.

To counter the modern nuclear-powered submarine, with its high underwater speed, most modern frigates are fitted with twinshaft gas turbine engines with controllable-pitch propellers. They must be at the cutting edge of naval technology, making their design and construction prohibitively costly for smaller navies, which usually prefer to buy them from larger countries.

France considered its frigates to be sloops, and used them mainly as gunboats to protect overseas interests, particularly guarding the approaches to the French nuclear test center at Mururoa Atoll in the Pacific.

During the Cold War, some European nations — the Netherlands and the former Federal German Republic, for example — cooperated in frigate design and construction, producing vessels to satisfy a common requirement. At the turn of the twenty-first century, France and Italy cooperated in developing the Horizon class frigate, which was first issued in 2008.

MODERN FRIGATES

HMS *Norfolk* was the lead ship of the Type 23 ("Iron Duke") class of frigates for the UK. Launched in 1987, like many frigates, the Type 23 was designed primarily for anti-

ANZAC TE KAHA: see page 29

INHAÚMA CLASS: see page 44

submarine warfare, but grew into a multirole design equipped for surface action as well as air defense. Vessels of this class are still in service with the UK, although *Norfolk* now serves in the Chilean navy as *Almirante Cochrane*. Anti-submarine armament consists of four torpedo tubes and a helicopter equipped with ASW weapons. *Norfolk* has a bow-mounted sonar and a towed sonar array for the sub-hunting role. It is also equipped with eight Harpoon anti-ship missiles and a vertical-launch system for Seawolf anti-air missiles. A general-purpose 114mm gun is

shipped, along with two 30mm cannon for close-in air defense. These can also be used against surface targets.

GENERAL WORKHORSE

Although optimized for anti-submarine warfare in the world's leading navies, frigates tend to be used as general purpose "workhorse" vessels in smaller navies. Only those that serve wealthier countries are customized for that nation's particular needs. Saudi Arabia, for example, purchased French Type F2000 class frigates in the

SACHSEN: see page 55

1980s and, in terms of capability and state-of-the-art electronic equipment, at the time of delivery these vessels could out-perform many of the frigates in service with countries in NATO and the Warsaw Pact.

Some smaller navies however, opt for small, light frigates armed with missiles. Since the end of the Cold War, Russia has offered many vessels for sale on the international arms market. Although Russian maritime technology in many areas is less sophisticated than the latest Western equipment, it is adequate for those Third World nations eager to secure naval superiority in their particular spheres of influence.

The US-built Oliver Hazard Perry class frigate is a general-purpose warship whose primary role is anti-submarine warfare and the escort of high-value assets such as amphibious assault ships, replenishment vessels and aircraft carriers. It also serves as a training ship for naval reservists. The O.H. Perry class was designed in the mid-1970s

LA FAYETTE: see page 49

F710

WEAPONS OF WAR

LCS INDEPENDENCE: see page 43

as a low-cost warship to replace the large numbers of World War II–era vessels that were due for retirement. The solution was to design and build an inexpensive vessel of modest capabilities, saving money for a small number of top-end combatants.

When the US commissioned the first ship of the Arleigh Burke class, in 1991, it was considered the most powerful surface warship ever built. In addition to the potent weapons it could deploy, this was the first ship equipped with an air-filtration system to cope against nuclear, biological, and chemical warfare.

The US is planning to introduce the first ship from the Zumwalt class in 2015, at an estimated cost of $3.45 billion. This warship is designed to be a multimission destroyer, with an emphasis on land attack. It will be armed with Tomahawk cruise missiles that have an operational range of up to 1,550 miles (2,500 km).

With constant technological innovation, and the numerous advantages and capabilities destroyers offer, they are certain to be a fixture in militaries around the world for years to come.

Álvaro de Bazán

F101

The Álvaro de Bazán class, also designated F-100, is an air defense vessel built around the Aegis system. It was the first European class and also the first frigate to carry Aegis. The lead ship of the class, *Álvaro de Bazán*, was commissioned in 2002. The vessels' primary role is fleet anti-air protection but they are also able to act as flagships for a task force in addition to the more usual frigate roles of anti-submarine and anti-surface warfare. Primary armament is the Evolved Sea Sparrow missile (ESSM) and Standard SM-2R anti-air missile. Harpoon anti-ship missiles are also carried and, in 2008, the Spanish government requested Tomahawk cruise missiles to arm its F-100 frigates.

SPECIFICATIONS

COUNTRY OF ORIGIN: Spain
TYPE: Frigate
LAUNCH DATE: October 2000
CREW: 250
DISPLACEMENT: 5708 tons (5800 tonnes) (full)
DIMENSIONS: 479 feet x 61 feet x 15 feet 10 inches (146.7 m x 18.6 m x 4.84 m)
ENDURANCE: 8334 miles (4500 nm) at 18 knots
MAIN ARMAMENT: 48-cell Mk 41 VLS for ESSM; 32xSM-2R; 8 x RGM-84 Harpoon; 1 x 127 mm Mk 45 mod 2 gun; 4 x 432 mm Mk 32 torpedo tubes; 1 x 20 mm CIWS on some vessels;
1 x helicopter
POWERPLANT: CODAG two GE LM2500 (34.8 MW; 46,646 hp); two Izar diesels (9 MW; 12,064 hp)
PERFORMANCE: 28.5 knots

Anzac Te Kaha

The ANZAC class was developed to meet the needs of the Australian and New Zealand navies, which included high capability in terms of air and missile defense. Out of many possible designs, a modified version of the German MEKO 200 class frigate was chosen, with the first vessel commissioning in 1996. Modular construction methods were used, allowing components to be built in several locations before being assembled. ANZAC class frigates have deployed in support of operations in Afghanistan and Iraq and are have received upgrades including mine and obstacle-avoidance sensors and improved anti-air weapons during their lives. Upgrades have included improved data transfer equipment and missile defenses, plus anti-ship missiles.

SPECIFICATIONS

COUNTRY OF ORIGIN: Australia and New Zealand
TYPE: Frigate
LAUNCH DATE: May 1996
CREW: 163
DISPLACEMENT: 3543 tons (3600 tonnes) (full)
DIMENSIONS: 387 feet x 48 feet 7 inches x 14 feet 3 inches (118 m x 14.8 m x 4.35 m)
ENDURANCE: 6000 nm (11,000 km) at 18 knots
MAIN ARMAMENT: 1 x Mk 5 Mod 41 VLS launching Evolved Sea Sparrow missiles (32) or 1 x 8-cell Sea Sparrow launcher in earlier vessels; 1 x 127 mm Mk 45 Mod 2 gun; 6 x 324 mm torpedo tubes launching Mk46 torpedoes; 1 x helicopter. Harpoon missiles to be fitted. Phalanx CIWS fitted to some vessels
POWERPLANT: CODOG one GE LM 2500 gas turbine delivering 30,159 hp (22.5 MW); two MTU 12V 1163 TB83 diesels delivering 8713 hp (6.5 MW) each
PERFORMANCE: 27 knots

Araguaya

Araguaya and her five sister ships were built to replace six British H-class destroyers which, under construction for Brazil, were taken over by the UK Navy at the outbreak of World War II. They followed the same design but used American equipment. All were built between 1943 and 1946 at the Ilha des Cobras Navy Yard. *Araguaya* was launched in 1946 and discarded in 1974. All the ships of this class were named after rivers, the others being the *Acre, Amazonas, Araguari, Apa,* and *Ajuricaba.* The original H-class destroyers destined for Brazil were to have been named *Jurua, Javary, Jutahy, Juruena, Jaguaribe,* and *Japarua.* They saw war service with the UK Navy as *Handy, Havant, Havelock, Hearty, Highlander,* and *Hurricane.* The H class destroyers were efficient, capable ships. Two of those taken over by the UK Navy, *Handy* and *Hurricane*, were lost in action.

SPECIFICATIONS

COUNTRY OF ORIGIN: Brazil
TYPE: Destroyer
LAUNCH DATE: November 20, 1943
CREW: 190
DISPLACEMENT: 1800 tons (1829 tonnes)
DIMENSIONS: 323 feet x 35 feet x 8 feet 6 inches (98.5 m x 10.7 m x 2.6 m)
ENDURANCE: 5000 nm (9265 km)
MAIN ARMAMENT: 4 x 127 mm guns; 2 x 40 mm guns
POWERPLANT: two-shaft geared turbines
PERFORMANCE: 35.5 knots

Arleigh Burke

This large class of guided-missile destroyers was designed to replace the ageing Adams- and Coontz-class destroyers that entered service in the early 1960s. The principal mission of the Arleigh Burke class is to provide effective anti-aircraft cover, for which they have the SPY 1D version of the Aegis area defense system. The Arleigh Burkes are the first US warships to be fully equipped for warfare in a nuclear, chemical, or biological environment, the crew being confined in a citadel located within the hull and superstructure. The ships are heavily protected; plastic Kevlar armor is fitted over all vital machinery and operations room spaces for this purpose. Armament includes one 127mm DP gun and two 20 mm (0.79 in) Phalanx CIWS mountings and the ships are fitted with a platform for an ASW helicopter. There is also a laser designator for the guidance of the DP gun's Deadeye shells.

SPECIFICATIONS

COUNTRY OF ORIGIN: United States
TYPE: Guided-missile destroyer
LAUNCH DATE: September 16, 1989
CREW: 303
DISPLACEMENT: 8400 tons (8534 tonnes)
DIMENSIONS: 266 feet 3 inches x 60 feet 1 inch x 30 feet (81 m x 18.3 m x 9.1 m)
ENDURANCE: 6000 nm (11,118 km)
MAIN ARMAMENT: Harpoon and Tomahawk anti-ship and land attack cruise missiles; 1 x 127 mm gun
POWERPLANT: twin-shaft gas turbine
PERFORMANCE: 32 knots

Brandenburg

The four Type 123 Brandenburg-class frigates (the others are *Schleswig-Holstein*, *Bayern,* and *Mecklenburg-Vorpommern*) were all commissioned between 1994 and 1996 and are based with the 6th Frigate Squadron of the German Navy at Wilhelmshaven. They were formerly known as the Deutschland class and were ordered in 1989 to replace the deleted Hamburg class. They are extremely well armed and carry a formidable array of electronic equipment, including air search D-band and air/sea search F-band radars. They are fitted with the Atlas Elektronik/ Paramax SATIR combat data system and their design, developed by Blohm und Voss, incorporates stealth technology. On-board space is allocated for a Task Group Commander and his battle staff. The ships of this class are optimized for combat in the relatively confined waters of the Baltic.

SPECIFICATIONS

COUNTRY OF ORIGIN: Germany
TYPE: Frigate
LAUNCH DATE: August 28, 1992
CREW: 199 plus 19 aircrew
DISPLACEMENT: 4775 tonnes (4700 tons)
DIMENSIONS: 455 feet 8 inches x 54 feet 9 inches x 22 feet 3 inches (138.9 m x 16.7 m x 6.8 m)
ENDURANCE: 3472 nm (6430 km)
MAIN ARMAMENT: 1 x 76 mm DP gun; 4 x Exocet; 16 x Sea Sparrow SAMs; 4 x 324 mm anti-submarine torpedo tubes
POWERPLANT: two shafts, two gas turbines, two diesels
PERFORMANCE: 29 knots

Bremen

A Germanized modification of the gas turbine-powered Dutch Kortenaer design, the eight-ship Bremen class of Type 122 frigates replaced the German Navy's elderly Fletcher-class destroyers and Kîln-class frigates. The first order was placed in 1977 and the first ship was commissioned in May 1982. The ships are fitted with fin stabilizers; a complete NBC defense citadel system is also fitted. The eight ships in service are the *Bremen* (F207), *Niedersachsen* (F208), *Rheinland-Pfalz* (F209), *Emden* (F210), *Kîln* (F211), *Karlsruhe* (F212), *Augsburg* (F213), and *Lübeck* (F214). Like the Brandenburgs, the Bremen class were intended for operations in the Baltic, but some units have been deployed farther afield in recent years. All have received an updated EW fit since 1994 and current plans call for them to remain in first-line service well into the twenty-first century.

SPECIFICATIONS

COUNTRY OF ORIGIN: Germany
TYPE: Frigate
LAUNCH DATE: September 27, 1979
CREW: 204
DISPLACEMENT: 2930 tons (2977 tonnes)
DIMENSIONS: 428 feet 1 inche x 47 feet 3 inches x 19 feet 7 inches (130.5 m x 14.4 m x 6 m)
ENDURANCE: 7000 nm (12,970 km)
MAIN ARMAMENT: 2 x quadruple Harpoon missile launchers; 1 x octuple NATO Sea Sparrow SAM launcher; 2 x RAM close-range SAM launchers; 1 x 76 mm gun; 4 x 324 mm torpedo tubes
POWERPLANT: two gas turbines, two diesels
PERFORMANCE: 32 knots

Dido

The 26-strong Leander class became the backbone of the UK Navy's frigate force during the 1960s and early 1970s. Vessels of this class followed the basic pattern of the Rothesay/Whitby class, but were more versatile and had improved fighting capabilities. *Dido*, launched in December 1961, was equipped with a powerful early-warning radar, a bow-mounted sonar, and variable-depth sonar. In addition to her gun and missile armament, it carried a triple-barrelled antisubmarine mortar. *Dido* also carried a Wasp light helicopter (later replaced by a Lynx), which could be equipped with anti-submarine homing torpedoes. Some ships in this class had their guns replaced by the Exocet sea-skimming missile, while others, *Dido* included, had their guns replaced by the Ikara anti-submarine missile system. Several nations bought Leanders, or built them under license.

SPECIFICATIONS

COUNTRY OF ORIGIN: United Kingdom
TYPE: Frigate
LAUNCH DATE: December 22, 1961
CREW: 263
DISPLACEMENT: 2800 tons (2844 tonnes)
DIMENSIONS: 371 feet 9 inches x 40 feet 8 inches x 17 feet 9 inches (113.3 m x 12.4 m x 5.4 m)
ENDURANCE: 4500 nm (8334 km)
MAIN ARMAMENT: 2 x 114 mm guns; 1 x quadruple launcher for Seacat SAMs
POWERPLANT: twin-screw turbines
PERFORMANCE: 30 knots

Downes

At the time of their building, the 46 Knox-class ocean escorts, of which *Downes* was one, comprised the largest group of destroyer-escort type warships built to the same design in the west since World War II. The ships were almost identical to the earlier Garcia and Brooke classes, but slightly larger. Original planning provided for the vessels to have the Sea Mauler, a short-range anti-aircraft missile adapted from a missile being developed by the US Army, but the Mauler/Sea Mauler program was abandoned because of technical difficulties. Mauler/Sea Mauler was a slim high-acceleration missile carried in a box of 12 and operated by a two-man crew; it could be used to spearhead amphibious assaults and engage low-flying aircraft. The ships had a very large superstructure and a distinctive cylindrical structure combining masts and engine exhaust stacks.

SPECIFICATIONS

COUNTRY OF ORIGIN: United States
TYPE: Frigate
LAUNCH DATE: December 13, 1969
CREW: 220
DISPLACEMENT: 4100 tons (4165 tonnes)
DIMENSIONS: 415 feet 4 inches x 46 feet 9 inches x 24 feet 7 inches (126.6 m x 14 m x 7.5 m)
ENDURANCE: 4500 nm (8338 km)
MAIN ARMAMENT: 1 x 127 mm gun; 1 x eight-tube Sea Sparrow missile launcher; Phalanx CIWS
POWERPLANT: single-screw, turbines
PERFORMANCE: 27 knots

Duguay-Trouin

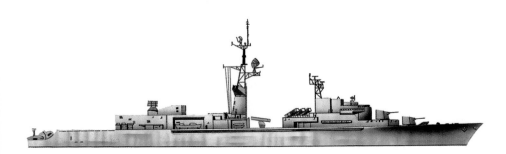

Duguay-Trouin was one of three vessels in a class that were designed to follow on from the earlier Aconite class destroyer. The single-screw propulsion of the earlier class had proved unsuccessful, leading to a doubling-up of the machinery in *Duguay-Trouin*. This resulted in an increase in speed of four knots. Helicopter facilities were included, plus essential backup, making the *Duguay-Trouin* and its sister vessels the first French warships of destroyer size to operate anti-submarine helicopters. The missile launcher is mounted forward of the funnel, which also carries the mast, with extensive magazines below. *Duguay-Trouin* was launched in June 1973. It was named after Admiral René Duguay-Trouin (1673–1736), who distinguished himself particularly in the wars of Louis XIV, was revered by his sailors, and died in virtual poverty.

SPECIFICATIONS

COUNTRY OF ORIGIN: France
TYPE: Destroyer
LAUNCH DATE: June 1, 1973
CREW: 250
DISPLACEMENT: 5800 tons (5892 tonnes)
DIMENSIONS: 500 feet 4 inches x 50 feet 2 inches x 21 feet 4 inches (152.5 m x 15.3 m x 6.5 m)
ENDURANCE: 5200 nm (9630 km)
MAIN ARMAMENT: 2 x 100 mm guns; 1 x eight-cell Crotale missile launcher
POWERPLANT: twin-screw, turbines
PERFORMANCE: 32 knots

Exeter

HMS Exeter, launched in April 1978 and commissioned in September 1980, is one of four Batch 2 Type 42 destroyers, the others being *Southampton, Nottingham,* and *Liverpool.* The Type 42s were originally designed to provide area defense for a task force with their British Aerospace Sea Dart surface-to-air missiles; these have a range of 21.5 nm (40 km) under radar or semi-active radar guidance and have a height envelope of 328–60,042 feet (100–18,300 m). The weapons also have a limited anti-ship capability. Generally, each Type 42 is armed with 22 Sea Dart rounds. The ships' Lynx helicopter carries the Sea Skua air-to-surface missile for use against lightly defended surface-ship targets, such as fast attack craft and has been operationally successful in the Falklands and Gulf conflicts, being especially effective against small, fast targets such as missile boats.

SPECIFICATIONS

COUNTRY OF ORIGIN: United Kingdom
TYPE: Destroyer
LAUNCH DATE: April 25, 1978
CREW: 253
DISPLACEMENT: 4100 tons (4166 tonnes)
DIMENSIONS: 410 feet 1 inch x 47 feet x 19 feet (125 m x 14.3 m x 5.8 m)
ENDURANCE: 3472 nm (6430 km)
MAIN ARMAMENT: 1 x 114 mm gun; Sea Dart SAM; 20 mm and Phalanx AA
POWERPLANT: twin shafts, four gas turbines
PERFORMANCE: 29 knots

Gatling

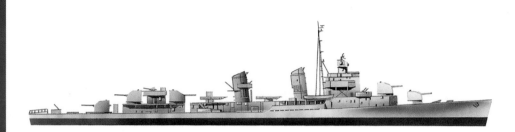

The USS *Gatling* was a Fletcher-class destroyer and, as such, was one of the largest classes built for the US Navy. Launched in June, 1943, it went into action in the Pacific in late January, 1944, when it formed part of a US naval task force attacking Japanese bases in the Marshall Islands. In June, 1944, *Gatling* was operating in support of US carriers attacking enemy bases in the Marianas and, in October of that same year, it was conducting similar operations off Formosa along with 13 other destroyers of Task Group 38.3. From December 30, 1944 to January 25, 1945, her Task Group carried out many attacks on Japanese airfields in the Central and Southwest Pacific and fought on to the Japanese surrender. A highly successful design, the Fletcher class formed the backbone of the Pacific Fleet. Many were sold after the war. *Gatling* was retired from the Navy in 1974.

SPECIFICATIONS

COUNTRY OF ORIGIN: United States
TYPE: Destroyer
LAUNCH DATE: June 20, 1943
CREW: 300
DISPLACEMENT: 2924 tons (2971 tonnes)
DIMENSIONS: 376 feet 5 inches x 39 feet 4 inches x 13 feet 9 inches (114.7 m x 12 m x 4. 2 m)
MAIN ARMAMENT: 5 x 127 mm (5 inches) guns
POWERPLANT: twin-screw turbines
PERFORMANCE: 37 knots

Glasgow

One of the first batch of Type 42 destroyers, HMS *Glasgow* was deployed to the South Atlantic in 1982 as part of the British task force assembled to retake the Falkland Islands. One of its sister ships, HMS *Sheffield*, was sunk by an Exocet missile launched by an Argentine Navy Super Etendard, while another, HMS *Coventry*, sustained three bomb hits on May 25 and sank within 45 minutes. Earlier, on May 12, the *Glasgow* itself had narrowly missed serious damage — and perhaps even destruction — when a bomb passed through its hull from side to side without exploding. The lack of any close-range air defense systems was a significant factor in each case and was one of many shortcomings caused by economic restraints. On the plus side, the ships' Sea Dart missiles were credited with the destruction of five enemy aircraft.

SPECIFICATIONS

COUNTRY OF ORIGIN: United Kingdom
TYPE: Destroyer
LAUNCH DATE: April 14, 1976
CREW: 253
DISPLACEMENT: 4100 tons (4165 tonnes)
DIMENSIONS: 410 feet 1 inch x 47 feet x 19 feet (125 m x 14.3 m x 5.8 m)
ENDURANCE: 4500 nm (8334 km)
MAIN ARMAMENT: 1 x 115 mm gun; 1 x twin Sea Dart launcher
POWERPLANT: twin-screw, gas turbines
PERFORMANCE: 30 knots

Grom

The *Grom* (Thunderbolt) was the former Russian Skory-class destroyer *Smetlivy*. This was the largest class of Soviet destroyers to be built after World War II and the ships, which were adapted from a pre-war design, incorporated many of the best design features of Germany's later destroyers. The other ex-Russian destroyer, the *Wicher* (Hurricane), was in fact the class prototype, the *Skory* herself. More than 70 Skory-class units were completed between 1950 and 1953. At a later date, the two Polish vessels were augmented by the transfer of a Kotlin-class destroyer. During the years of the Cold War, the Polish Navy, as a satellite of the Soviet Union, would have had an important part to play in operations in the Baltic. By the early 1980s, its strength was centred on fast-attack craft and patrol boats, together with five submarines, all supplied by the Soviet Union.

SPECIFICATIONS

COUNTRY OF ORIGIN: Soviet Union/Poland
TYPE: Destroyer
LAUNCH DATE: November 17, 1951
CREW: 280
DISPLACEMENT: 3100 tons (3150 tonnes)
DIMENSIONS: 395 feet 4 inches x 38 feet 9 inches x 15 feet (120.5 m x 11.8 m x 4.6 m)
ENDURANCE: 3800 nm (7037 km)
MAIN ARMAMENT: 4 x 130 mm guns; 2 x 76 mm AA guns
POWERPLANT: twin-screws, turbines
PERFORMANCE: 36 knots

Gurkha

Launched in 1960, *Gurkha* was one of seven general-purpose frigates in the Tribal class. These vessels were among the first ships to be fully air-conditioned in all crew areas and most working spaces. The standard steam turbine developed 12,500 hp (9321 kW) and this could be boosted by a gas turbine which increased output to 20,000 hp (14,914 kW). The ships were very seaworthy and made good speed even in unfavorable sea states. Of the ships in this class, *Ashanti*, *Eskimo,* and *Gurkha* were ordered in 1955-56, *Nubian* and *Tartar* under the 1956–57 program, and *Mohawk* and *Zulu* under the 1957–58 program. The ships were of welded prefabricated construction and were all completed between 1961 and 1964. They were the first frigates designed to carry a helicopter for anti-submarine reconnaissance.

SPECIFICATIONS

COUNTRY OF ORIGIN: United Kingdom
TYPE: Frigate
LAUNCH DATE: July 11, 1960
CREW: 253
DISPLACEMENT: 2700 tons (2743 tonnes)
DIMENSIONS: 357 feet 7 inches x 42 feet x 17 feet 6 inches (109 m x 12.8 m x 5.3 m)
ENDURANCE: 4200 nm (7778 km)
MAIN ARMAMENT: 2 x 114 mm guns; 1 x Limbo three-barrelled anti-submarine mortar
POWERPLANT: single-screw, turbine and gas turbine
PERFORMANCE: 28 knots

H

Hamayuki

The modern Japanese Navy is a well-handled, efficient fighting force, the core of its strength being submarines, destroyers, and frigates. *Hamayuki* was a radical departure from previous Japanese anti-submarine destroyer designs. Although the weapons systems are of US origin, the concept and general layout closely resemble the successful French Georges Leygues class. The British propulsion machinery consists of two groups of gas turbines, one set developing 56,780 hp (42,341 kW), the other 10,680 hp (7964 kW). *Hamayuki* is one of 12 guided-missile destroyers of the Hatsuyuki class. *Shirayuki* was the first to be fitted with the Phalanx CIWS, early in 1992 and all the other ships had been retrofitted by 1996. The last three of the class — *Setoyuki, Asayuki,* and *Shimayuki* — are equipped with the Canadian Beartrap landing aid. All vessels carry the Sikorsky SH-60J Seahawk.

SPECIFICATIONS

COUNTRY OF ORIGIN: Japan
TYPE: Destroyer
LAUNCH DATE: May 27, 1982
CREW: 250
DISPLACEMENT: 3700 tons (3760 tonnes)
DIMENSIONS: 432 feet x 45 feet x 13 feet 9 inches (131.7 m x 13.7 m x 4.2 m)
ENDURANCE: 5000 nm (9260 km)
MAIN ARMAMENT: 1 x 76 mm gun; 1 x eight-cell Sea Sparrow launcher; 2 x Phalanx CIWS
POWERPLANT: twin screws, gas turbines
PERFORMANCE: 30 knots

Independence (LCS)

An alternative design of Littoral Combat Ship, USS *Independence* uses a trimaran hull, rather than the more conventional single hull of USS *Freedom*. Like *Freedom*, *Independence* carries a set of core systems that can be augmented by mission packages to tailor the vessel to whatever mission is required. Light armored vehicles such as the Stryker can be carried in the mission bay and two helicopters are supported on the flight deck, enabling the vessel to act as a transport or support ship. The development of littoral combat ships is ongoing, with changing requirements and the experimental nature of the vessels causing the project to be re-evaluated at intervals.

SPECIFICATIONS
COUNTRY OF ORIGIN: United States
TYPE: Combat ship
LAUNCH DATE: December 2009
CREW: 40 plus mission personnel
DISPLACEMENT: 2740 tons (2784 tonnes) (full)
DIMENSIONS: 418 feet x 103.7 feet x 13 feet (127.5 m x 31.6 m x 3.96 m)
ENDURANCE: 4800 nm (8890 km) at 18 knots
MAIN ARMAMENT: 1 x 57 mm gun, 4 x 12.7 mm machine guns, 1 x SeaRAM launcher
POWERPLANT: two General Electric LM2500 gas turbines; two MTU Friedrichshafen 20V 8000 series diesels
PERFORMANCE: 44 knots

Inhaúma

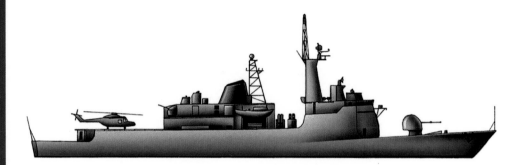

Inhaúma is the lead ship of a class of four corvettes designed by the Brazilian Naval Design Office with the assistance of the German privately-owned Marine Technik design company. *Inhaúma* was commissioned in December 1989, followed by the other corvettes between 1991 and 1994. Originally, it had been intended to order a class of 16 ships, but this was reduced to four because of financial considerations. As a country with a long coastline, Brazil has always endeavored to maintain a substantial navy. Its first warship, built in the UK in 1907, came about as a response to the growth of the Argentine Navy and, as a consequence, Brazil had ships of this type in commission even before larger powers such as France, Italy, and Russia. Corvettes such as *Inhaúma* are ideally suited to the task of defending Brazil's lengthy coast.

SPECIFICATIONS
COUNTRY OF ORIGIN: Brazil
TYPE: Corvette
LAUNCH DATE: December 13, 1986
CREW: 122
DISPLACEMENT: 1970 tons (2002 tonnes)
DIMENSIONS: 314 feet 2 inches x 37 feet 5 inches x 12 feet 1 inches (95.83 m x 11.4 m x 3.7 m)
ENDURANCE: 3474 nm (6434 km)
MAIN ARMAMENT: 1 x 115 mm gun; Exocet SSMs; 6 x 324 mm torpedo tubes
POWERPLANT: two shafts, one gas turbine, two diesels
PERFORMANCE: 27 knots

Knox class

The Knox class is similar to the Garcia and Brooke designs from which it is developed, but is slightly larger because of the use of non-pressure fired boilers. It was designed in the early 1960s. The first vessels entered US Navy service in 1969, the last units of the 46-strong class being delivered in 1974. They are specialized ASW ships and have been heavily criticized because of their single propeller and solitary 127mm gun armament. A five-ship class based on the Knox design, but with a Mk22 missile launcher for 16 standard SM-1MR missiles, was built for the Spanish Navy. Knox-class frigates have been used over the years to test individual prototype weapon and sensor systems, such as the Phalanx close-range anti-aircraft system. Some units were assigned to the US Naval Reserve Force in the late 1980s as replacements for ageing destroyers.

SPECIFICATIONS

COUNTRY OF ORIGIN: United States
TYPE: Frigate
LAUNCH DATE: November 19, 1966
CREW: 283
DISPLACEMENT: 3877 tons (3939 tonnes)
DIMENSIONS: 438 feet x 46 feet 10 inches x 15 feet 1 inch (133.5 m x 14.3 m x 4.6 m)
ENDURANCE: 5000 nm (9260 km)
MAIN ARMAMENT: 1 x 127 mm DP gun; SAMs; ASW and anti-ship missiles
POWERPLANT: geared steam turbines
PERFORMANCE: 27 knots

Kongo

The *Kongo* was commissioned in March, 1983, and was followed by four more vessels of her class, the *Kirishima*, *Myoko,* and *Choukai*, the latter being commissioned in March 1998. The ships are larger and improved versions of the US's Arleigh Burke destroyers and are armed with a lightweight version of the Aegis air defense system. As well as providing area air defense for the fleet, the ships also contribute towards the air defense of mainland Japan, standing well out from the Home Islands in the role of air defense picket ships. Although designated as destroyers, the vessels are in fact cruiser size. Their entry into Japanese Navy service was slowed down by a combination of cost and the reluctance of the US Congress to release Aegis technology. The highly sophisticated Aegis is the US Navy's primary air defense system.

SPECIFICATIONS

COUNTRY OF ORIGIN: Japan
TYPE: Destroyer
LAUNCH DATE: September 26, 1991
CREW: 307
DISPLACEMENT: 9485 tons (9637 tonnes)
DIMENSIONS: 528 feet 2 inches x 68 feet 11 inches x
32 feet 9 inches (161 m x 21 m x 10 m)
ENDURANCE: 3908 nm (7238 km)
MAIN ARMAMENT: 1 x 127 mm gun; Harpoon SSM;
Standard SAM; 6 x 324 mm torpedo tubes; vertical
launch ASROC
POWERPLANT: two shafts, four gas turbines
PERFORMANCE: 30 knots

Krivak II class

In 1970, the first unit of the Krivak I class of large anti-submarine warfare vessel entered service with the Soviet Navy. Built at the Zhdanov shipyard in Leningrad, the Kaliningrad shipyard and the Kamysh-Burun shipyard in Kerch between 1971 and 1982, 21 units of this version were constructed. In 1976 the Krivak II class — of which 11 were built at Kaliningrad between that year and 1981 — was first seen. This differed from the previous class in having single 100 mm guns substituted for the twin 76 mm turrets of the earlier version and a larger, variable-depth sonar at the stern. Both classes were re-rated to patrol ship status in the late 1970s, possibly in the light of what some Western observers considered to be deficiencies in terms of limited endurance for ASW operations in open waters. Nevertheless, the Krivak IIs caused some consternation in NATO circles when they first appeared.

SPECIFICATIONS

COUNTRY OF ORIGIN: Russia
TYPE: Frigate
LAUNCH DATE: 1975 (Rezvyy)
CREW: 220
DISPLACEMENT: 3700 tons (3759 tonnes)
DIMENSIONS: 405 feet 2 inches x 45 feet 11 inches x 15 feet 5 inches (123.5 m x 14 m x 4.7 m)
ENDURANCE: 2800 nm (5188 km)
MAIN ARMAMENT: 2 x single 100 mm DP guns; SAMs; ASW missiles; 8 x 533 mm torpedo tubes
POWERPLANT: two shafts, four gas turbines
PERFORMANCE: 32 knots

La Fayette

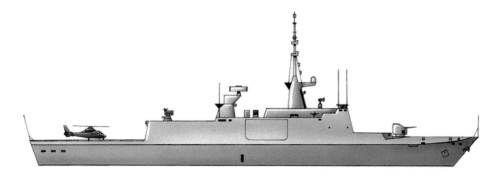

The first three of five La Fayette-class frigates were ordered in July 1988, but construction was delayed because of funding problems. *La Fayette* was commissioned in March, 1996, and *Surcouf* and *Courbet* in February and March, 1997, respectively. *Aconit* had a commission date of December, 1999, and *Guepratte* of January, 2002. The La Fayette class-frigates are intended for out-of-area operations on overseas stations, and the first three are assigned to the Indian Ocean. Super Frelon helicopters may be operated from the flight deck and the vessels can launch inflatable boats from a hatch in the stern that hinges upwards. The ships incorporate many stealth features and extensive use is made of radar absorbent paint. Protruding equipment such as capstans and bollards are either hidden or fitted as flush as possible.

SPECIFICATIONS

COUNTRY OF ORIGIN: France
TYPE: Frigate
LAUNCH DATE: June 13, 1992
CREW: 139
DISPLACEMENT: 3600 tons (3658 tonnes)
DIMENSIONS: 407 feet 6 inches x 50 feet 6 inches x 19 feet 5 inches (124.2 m x 15.4 m x 5.9 m)
ENDURANCE: 7812 nm (14,467 km)
MAIN ARMAMENT: 1 x 100 mm DP gun; Exocet SSM; Crotale SAM
POWERPLANT: two shafts, four diesel engines
PERFORMANCE: 25 knots

Neustrashimy

There were originally intended to be three frigates in the Neustrashimy class, but the third was launched in July 1993 with only the hull completed and was scrapped in mid-1997 without any further work being done. *Neustrashimy* was launched in May, 1988, and began her sea trials in the Baltic in December, 1990, being commissioned in January, 1993. The second unit, *Yaroslavl Mudry*, was commissioned in 1998 and may be offered for sale. Both ships were built at Kaliningrad. They are slightly larger than the Krivak class and each has a helicopter, following the pattern set by Western anti-submarine frigates. The ships have the same propulsion units as the Udaloy II class. Both were assigned to the Baltic Fleet in 1999. Attempts have been made to incorporate stealth features into these vessels, though with what degree of success it is not known.

SPECIFICATIONS

COUNTRY OF ORIGIN: Russia
TYPE: Frigate
LAUNCH DATE: May 1, 1988
CREW: 210
DISPLACEMENT: 4250 tons (4318 tonnes)
DIMENSIONS: 430 feet 5 inches x 50 feet 10 inches x 15 feet 9 inches (131.2 m x 15.5 m x 4.8 m)
ENDURANCE: 3908 nm (7238 km)
MAIN ARMAMENT: combined 30 mm gun and SA-N-11 SAM system; fitted for SS-N-25 SSM; SA-N-9 SAM; 6 x 533 mm torpedo tubes; A/S mortars
POWERPLANT: two shafts, four gas turbines
PERFORMANCE: 30 knots

Niteroi

Of the seven ships in the Niteroi class, four (*Niteroi, Defensora, Constituicao,* and *Liberal*) were built in the UK by Vosper Thorneycroft Ltd. The others, *Independencia, União*, and *Brasil* were built at the Arsenal de Marinha yards in Rio de Janeiro. The ships were based on Vosper's Mk10 frigate design, which, fitted with a combined diesel or gas turbine propulsion plant, is considered to be exceptionally economical in terms of manpower when compared with previous warships of this size. The class was being upgraded in the late 1990s, modifications including the replacement of Seacat with the Aspide SAM system. The vessels carry the Westland Super Lynx helicopter, which is armed with the Sea Skua ASM. All are based at Niteroi and form the Brazilian Navy's First Frigate Squadron, which is the Brazilian Navy's premier surface attack unit.

SPECIFICATIONS

COUNTRY OF ORIGIN: Brazil
TYPE: Frigate
LAUNCH DATE: February 8, 1974
CREW: 217
DISPLACEMENT: 3707 tons (3766 tonnes)
DIMENSIONS: 424 feet x 44 feet 2 inches x 18 feet 2 inches (129.2 m x 13.5 m x 5.5 m)
ENDURANCE: 4600 nm (8524 km)
MAIN ARMAMENT: 1 or 2 x 115 mm guns; Exocet SSM; Seacat SAM; Ikara ASW system
POWERPLANT: two shafts, two gas turbines, four diesels
PERFORMANCE: 30 knots

Oliver Hazard Perry

The USS *Oliver Hazard Perry* was the first of a class of 55 general-purpose frigates designed to escort merchant convoys or amphibious squadrons. Their primary role was to provide area defense of surface forces against attacking aircraft and cruise missiles, with anti-surface warfare as a secondary role. Because of cost considerations, the first 26 ships were not retrofitted to carry two LAMPS III ASW helicopters, as originally planned, but retained the LAMPS I. LAMPS facilities include the Recovery Assistance, Security and Traversing (RAST) system, which allows the launch and recovery of the Sikorsky SH-60 helicopters with the ship rolling through 28 degrees and pitching up to 5 degrees. Two ships of this class, the *Stark* and *Samuel B. Roberts*, were damaged in missile attacks while patrolling the Persian Gulf during the Iraq-Iran war in 1987 and 1988.

SPECIFICATIONS

COUNTRY OF ORIGIN: United States
TYPE: Frigate
LAUNCH DATE: September 25, 1976
CREW: 215
DISPLACEMENT: 3658 tons (3717 tonnes)
DIMENSIONS: 445 feet x 45 feet x 14 feet 10 inches (135.6 m x 13.7 m x 4.5 m)
ENDURANCE: 5600 nm (10,371 km)
MAIN ARMAMENT: 1 x 76 mm DP gun; 2 x triple 324 mm torpedo tubes; Harpoon SSMs and Standard ASMs
POWERPLANT: single shaft, two gas turbines
PERFORMANCE: 29 knots

Perth

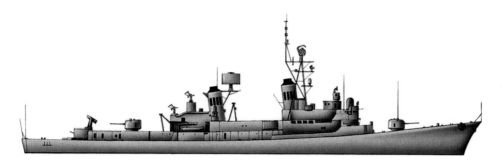

Australia's three Perth-class guided-missile destroyers (the others are the *Hobart* and *Brisbane*) were modified vessels of the American Charles F. Adams class, all commissioned in the mid-1960s. The ships have since undergone several updates; *Perth* was first modernized in 1974 in the US, when standard missiles, replacement gun mountings, a new combat data system, and modern radars were fitted. *Hobart* and *Brisbane* were brought up to the same standard in 1978 and 1979 at the Garden Island Dockyard in Sydney. A further upgrade was carried out between 1987 and 1991, with all ships receiving the Phalanx CIWS, new search and fire control radars, decoy and ECM equipment, and the new Mk13 missile launcher for the Harpoon SSM. All three ships were decommissioned between 1999 and 2001.

SPECIFICATIONS

COUNTRY OF ORIGIN: United States/Australia
TYPE: Destroyer
LAUNCH DATE: September 26, 1963
CREW: 310
DISPLACEMENT: 4618 tons (4692 tonnes)
DIMENSIONS: 440 feet 9 inches x 47 feet 1 inch x 20 feet 1 inche (134.3 m x 14.3 m x 6.1 m)
ENDURANCE: 5210 nm (9650 km)
MAIN ARMAMENT: 2 x 127 mm guns; Phalanx CIWS; Harpoon SSM; Standard SAM; 6 x 324 mm torpedo tubes
POWERPLANT: two shafts, two geared steam turbines
PERFORMANCE: 30+ knots

Prat

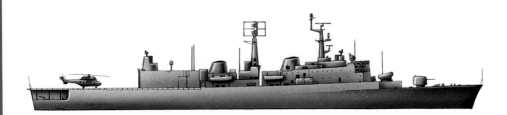

The use of British warships is traditional in the Chilean Navy. The Chilean Navy's former British Navy County-class destroyers, *Prat* (ex-*Norfolk*), *Cochrane* (ex-*Antrim*), *Latorre* (ex-*Glamorgan*), and *Blanco Encalada* (ex-*Fife*) were transferred from the UK between April, 1982, and August, 1987, extensive refits being carried out after transfer. All are named after senior officers, but the titles *Almirante* and *Capitan* were not used. In 1988, *Blanco Encalada* was converted as a helicopter carrier for two Super Pumas, *Cochrane* being similarly converted in 1994. The two remaining vessels served as flagships. All four ships were fitted with the Israeli Barak I short-range SAM system. The ships were removed from service between 1998-2006.

SPECIFICATIONS

COUNTRY OF ORIGIN: United Kingdom/Chile
TYPE: Destroyer
LAUNCH DATE: November 16, 1967
CREW: 470
DISPLACEMENT: 6200 tons (6299 tonnes)
DIMENSIONS: 520 feet 6 inches x 54 feet x 20 feet 6 inches (158.7 m x 16.5 m x 6.3 m)
ENDURANCE: 3038 nm (5620 km)
MAIN ARMAMENT: 2 x 115 mm guns; Exocet SSM; Seaslug and Barak SAM; 6 x 324 mm torpedo tubes
POWERPLANT: two shafts, two geared steam turbines, four gas turbines
PERFORMANCE: 30 knots

Sachsen

The Sachsen class is a primarily anti-air frigate built as part of a cooperative endeavor between Germany, Spain, and the Netherlands. Three vessels are in service. The Sachsen class uses a Combined Diesel and Gas Turbine (CODAG) propulsion system optimized for economical cruising, but capable of high speeds when using both diesel and gas turbine propulsion. Primary armament consists of vertically launched medium-range anti-aircraft missiles, with shorter range missiles and two 27mm cannon for point defense, backed up by decoy launchers. An advanced 155mm gun has been demonstrated aboard one vessel of the class, necessitating specially developed mountings. Two helicopters are carried for anti-submarine warfare and utility work, with an advanced computer controlled system to assist landings.

SPECIFICATIONS

COUNTRY OF ORIGIN: Germany
TYPE: Frigate
LAUNCH DATE: July 2003
CREW: 230 crew; + 13 aircrew
DISPLACEMENT: 6272 tons (5690 tonnes)
DIMENSIONS: 469 feet 2 inches x 57 feet 1 inch x 16 feet 5 inches (143 m x 17.4 m x 5 m)
ENDURANCE: more than 4000 nm (7400 km) at 18 knots (33 km/h)
MAIN ARMAMENT: 1 x MK. 41 VLS Tactical with 8 cells for 32 RIM-162 ESSM and 24 SM- 2 IIIA surface-to-air missiles; 2 x RAM launchers with 21 surface-to- air/ CIWS-missiles each; 2 x quadruple Harpoon missile launchers; 1 x OTO-Melara 76 mm dual-purpose gun; 2 x Mauser MLG 27 27 mm autocannons; 2 x triple torpedo launchers
POWERPLANT: CODAG; two propeller shafts, controllable pitch propellers; two MTU V20 diesel engines, 9919 hp (7.4 MW) each; one General Electric LM2500 gas turbine
PERFORMANCE: 29+ knots

Spruance

Built as replacements for the numerous Gearing-class destroyers, the 31 ships of the Spruance class are arguably the most capable anti-submarine warfare vessels ever built. Constructed by the modular assembly technique, whereby large sections of the hull are built in various parts of the shipyard and then welded together on the slipway, these were the first large US warships to employ all gas turbine propulsion. The successful hull design of the Spruance-class destroyers was used, with modifications, on two other classes of US warship and has reduced rolling and pitching tendencies, thus providing a better weapons platform. All vessels in the Spruance class have undergone major weapons changes over the years. At least nine Spruance-class warships supported the various Battle Groups during the Gulf War in 1991.

SPECIFICATIONS

COUNTRY OF ORIGIN: United States
TYPE: Torpedo boat
LAUNCH DATE: November 10, 1973
CREW: 15
DISPLACEMENT: 31 tons (31 tonnes)
DIMENSIONS: 95 feet 2 inches x 11 feet 6 inches x 3 feet (29 m x 3.5 m x 0.9 m)
ENDURANCE: not known
MAIN ARMAMENT: none when first completed
POWERPLANT: single screw, vertical compound engine
PERFORMANCE: 18.2 knots

Type 052B Guangzhou

The Guangzhou class multirole destroyer shows Russian influences and indeed contains Russian-designed systems. When the first of the two-vessel class entered service in 2004, it was the first Chinese destroyer with significant air defense capability. A 100mm gun is carried in a single mount on the foredeck and is able to engage air and surface targets as well as some missiles. Long-range anti-ship missiles are carried, which can receive mid-course guidance from the destroyer's Kamov helicopter. Torpedoes and rocket launchers give the vessels an anti-submarine capability. The overall design is not a "stealth ship" as such, but incorporates low-observable features and technologies designed to reduce thermal and radar signature. These vessels represent a significant increase in the "Blue Water" capability of the Chinese navy, i.e. its ability to operate effectively in the open ocean.

SPECIFICATIONS

COUNTRY OF ORIGIN: China
TYPE: Destroyer
LAUNCH DATE: May 2002
CREW: 280
DISPLACEMENT: 7716 tons (7000 tonnes)
DIMENSIONS: 505 feet 3 inches x 55 feet 8 inches x 19 feet 8 inches (154 m x 17 m x 6 m)
ENDURANCE: not known
MAIN ARMAMENT: 16 x YJ-83 anti-ship missiles; 48 x SA-N-12 Grizzly surface-to-air missiles; 1 x dual purpose gun; 2 x Type 730 CIWS; two anti-submarine mortars; 6 x torpedo tubes; 1 x Kamov Ka-27 helicopter
POWERPLANT: CODOG; 57,000 hp (42.5 MW)
PERFORMANCE: 30 knots

Type F2000

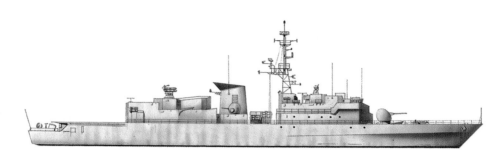

Although optimized for anti-submarine warfare in the world's leading navies, frigates tend to be used as general-purpose "workhorse" vessels in smaller navies. Only those that serve wealthier countries have the benefit of custom-built ships. France has proved extremely adept at exporting naval hardware to Middle East countries. A good example of this is Saudi Arabia, which purchased Type F2000 class frigates from France in the 1980s. In terms of capability and equipment, these vessels, at the time of their delivery, could out-perform many of the frigates in service with NATO and the Warsaw Pact, with particular regard to their state-of-the art electronic equipment. The weapon systems are predominantly French in origin, although the SSMs are the Franco-Italian Otomat rather than the Exocet. A Dauphin helicopter is carried for ASW work.

SPECIFICATIONS

COUNTRY OF ORIGIN: France/Saudi Arabia
TYPE: Frigate
LAUNCH DATE: April 23, 1983
CREW: 179
DISPLACEMENT: 2610 tons (2652 tonnes)
DIMENSIONS: 377 feet 4 inches x 41 feet x 15 feet 5 inches (115 m x 12.5 m x 4.7 m)
ENDURANCE: 5000 nm (9265 km)
MAIN ARMAMENT: 1 x 100 mm DP and 2 x 40 mm AA guns; Otomat SSMs; Crotale SAMs; 4 x 533 mm and 2 x 324 mm torpedo tubes
POWERPLANT: twin shafts, four diesel engines
PERFORMANCE: 30 knots

Udaloy

The Udaloy class of large anti-submarine-warfare destroyers was originally designated BalCom 3 (Baltic Combatant No 3) by NATO. The original seven ships, all operational by 1987, were *Udaloy, Vitse Admiral Kulakov, Marshal Vasilievsky, Admiral Zakorov, Admiral Spiridinov, Admiral Tributs,* and *Marshal Shaposhnikov. Udaloy* herself achieved Initial Operational Capability (IOC) in 1981. The vessels of the Udaloy class are similar to the US Spruance-class destroyers, even to the use of gas turbine propulsion. Each Udaloy can carry two Ka-27 Helix helicopters and they were the first Russian destroyers to have this capability. All Udaloy units were built at either the Yantar shipyard in Kaliningrad or the Zhdanov shipyard in Leningrad (St Petersburg). The vessels are reported to be extremely capable in their designed role.

SPECIFICATIONS

COUNTRY OF ORIGIN: Russia
TYPE: Destroyer
LAUNCH DATE: February 5, 1980
CREW: 300
DISPLACEMENT: 8200 tons (8332 tonnes)
DIMENSIONS: 531 feet 6 inches x 63 feet 4 inches x 20 feet 4 inches (162 m x 19.3 m x 6.2 m)
ENDURANCE: 12,500 nm (23,162 km)
MAIN ARMAMENT: 2 x 100 mm guns; SS-N-14 ASW missiles; SA-N-9 SAMs; 8 x 533 mm torpedo tubes
POWERPLANT: two shafts, four gas turbines
PERFORMANCE: 34 knots

DESTROYERS

1945 TO TODAY

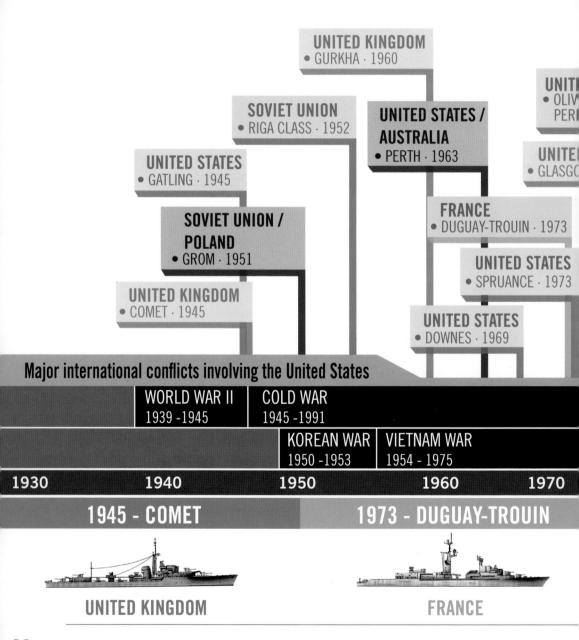

UNITED KINGDOM
- GURKHA · 1960

SOVIET UNION
- RIGA CLASS · 1952

UNITED STATES / AUSTRALIA
- PERTH · 1963

UNIT[...]
- OLIV[...]
  PER[...]

UNITED STATES
- GATLING · 1945

UNITE[...]
- GLASG[...]

FRANCE
- DUGUAY-TROUIN · 1973

SOVIET UNION / POLAND
- GROM · 1951

UNITED STATES
- SPRUANCE · 1973

UNITED KINGDOM
- COMET · 1945

UNITED STATES
- DOWNES · 1969

Major international conflicts involving the United States

	WORLD WAR II	COLD WAR		
	1939 -1945	1945 -1991		
		KOREAN WAR	VIETNAM WAR	
		1950 -1953	1954 - 1975	
1930	1940	1950	1960	1970

1945 - COMET

1973 - DUGUAY-TROUIN

UNITED KINGDOM

FRANCE

FEATURED WEAPONS TIMELINE

This timeline features notable advancements in
military technologies by influential nations worldwide.

**FRANCE /
SAUDI ARABIA**
- TYPE F2000 · 1983

TATES
AZARD
976

SOVIET UNION
- NEUSTRASHIMY · 1988

NGDOM
976

FRANCE
- LA FAYETTE · 1992

UNITED STATES
- INDEPENDENCE · 2009

GERMANY
BREMEN · 1979

UNITED STATES
- ARLEIGH BURKE · 1989

CHINA
- TYPE 052B
  GUANGZHOU · 2002

JAPAN
- HAMAYUKI · 1982

GERMANY
- SACHSEN · 2003

AFGHANISTAN WAR
2001 - PRESENT

PERSIAN GULF
WAR 1990 -1991

IRAQ WAR
2003 - 2011

| 1980 | 1990 | 2000 | 2010 |

1982 - HAMAYUKI

2009 - INDEPENDENCE

JAPAN

UNITED STATES

Glossary

amphibious vessels
can be used on land and in water

anti-air warfare
detecting and avoiding or neutralizing hostile
air units

anti-submarine warfare
the set of techniques, sensors, and weapons used to
locate enemy submarines and destroy them

anti-submarine rocket launcher
a shipboard system that fires rockets at submarines

armament
the weapons and supplies of war that equip a
military unit

casualties
the injured, killed, captured, or missing personnel
in action with an enemy

commission
to put a ship into active service

deployment
the distribution of military forces in preparation
for battle

doctrine
a military doctrine defines ethics in campaigns,
battles, and engaging with the enemy

echolocation
process that determines the shape, size, and
distance of an object based on the sound waves
generated and received

Falkands War
a war fought in 1982 due to Argentina's invasion of
the British-owned Falkland Islands

hull
the hollow, watertight lowermost portion of a ship
that is partially submerged and supports the ship

mines
an explosive device placed in the ocean to destroy
ships or submarines

nuclear warhead
an explosive weapon that gets its destructive force
from a nuclear reaction

procurement
the acquisition of technologies, programs,
and products

propulsion
a force that causes movement

refit
make repairs, which often requires adding new parts,
to make a vessel ready for use

SONAR (Sound Navigation and Ranging)
a method for detecting and locating objects
submerged in water by echolocation

Further Information

Websites

http://usmilitary.about.com/library/milinfo/navyfacts/bldestroyers.htm
This site offers information on the background and features of a destroyer.

http://www.militaryfactory.com/armor/index.asp
Find out about the history of destroyers, from early ships to modern aircraft carriers.

www.mvpa.org/
The Military Vehicle Preservation Association is an international organization dedicated to the collection and restoration of historic military vehicles.

www.mvtf.org/
See one of the largest collections of historical military vehicles, overseen by the Military Vehicle Technology Foundation.

Books

Cooke, Tim. *Warships*. Smart Apple Media, 2013.
An up-close look at military ships used throughout history.

Rustad, Martha E. *U.S. Navy Cruisers*. Capstone Press, 2006.
An inside look at the ships used by the Navy, including details on their design, function, and mission.

Jackson, Robert. *The Encyclopedia of Warships: From World War II to the Present Day.* Summertime Publishing, 2006.
An informative book on destroyers in World War II, the Cold War, and the modern era.

Tomajczyk, Steve. *Modern U. S. Navy Destroyers*. MBI Publishing Company, 2001.
Learn about the ship's advanced sonar system, its powerful weapons, and a launch system.

Index of Destroyers Profile Pages